TRACING THE LINE

A Collection of Poems

HARRY LAFNEAR

Harry Lafnear

PROSODYETC.

ISBN-10: 1461042992
ISBN-13: 978-1461042990

First edition, POD, May 2011

Literature. Poetry. Lafnear, Harry. Tracing the Line.

PRODUCED BY PROSODYETC.

www.prosodyetc.com

For manuscript submission guidelines, contact
publish@prosodyetc.com.

For inquiries to the author, contact
hlafnear@gmail.com.

ACKNOWLEDGMENTS

The author thanks Jerry Dyer and Pushpa MacFarlane.
But for their keen editorial diligence, this book would
bite off your fingers.

The following works have been previously published:

Via *The Everyday Muse*—"Aunt Nora's Gift to Poetry," "The
Benefits of Rain," "Catering to the Muse," "Dinner Belles,"
"Exploring Heaven," "First Hunger," "The Flight of Words,"
"Like Breathing," "The Lion on the Bus," "Mew,"
"Odometer," "Opportunity for a Poem," "Purpleclip,"
"Representing America," "Sabbatical," "Spring Lambs,"
"Straightjacket," "Surrendering September," "That Time,"
"There I Will Shine," "The Tide," "Vacation," and "The
Whispers of Wolves;"

Via *IndieFeed Performance Poetry*—"The Flight of Words;"

Via Nils Peterson's Poet Laureate blog, Santa Clara
County—"Mission College Carpool."

Cover and interior design by Harry Lafnear.

To Dennis *&* Christine Richardson,

And all the other lofty souls
who make the Willow Glen readings
such a dependable joy.

Contents

Writers

& Other Curious Beasts

ACTORS

Like Breathing

Think of each breath.
Lead it like a lion on a leash.
Say to it, *come here*,
Then wait, hiding anticipation
While it fails to obey.

Command it again,
As if it was a given,
As if there was no fear.
In. Breath in.
And feel it finally yield
With a reluctance that belies
All reason.

There is no ease,
No patience, no safety.
Out. Breath out.
The whole while
Longing for *in* again,
Too ready for reverse.

Think of it even as you sleep,
Waking up breathless,
The lion on your chest,
Whenever you forget to dream
Of how easy it should be.

Going Ahead

I am ready
To fling open the moving door of this day,
Pound on the pavement
The soles of a plan,
Dive in through the garrison window
And tackle one possibility
While the others sound the alarm.

I am ready
To haul home this shifting notion,
Shine a naked lamp in its eyes,
Break it with rubber hoses and waterboarding,
And make it tell me lies about tomorrow,
Already on the run, when
The day glares back.

Go ahead, it says,
I am ready too.

Hide and Seek

Listening is
The key to finding stillness on the tread-worried walk,
The quiet that doesn't quite belong on the wind,
The kiss blown from the sheltering void
Sitting watch with the stars.

Listening is
The lock set deep within the walls of noise,
The almost forgotten sigh of the trees,
The hum newly remembered on the rolling road,
The hiss thrown from the quivering rush
Counting time in the blood.

Listening is
The contradiction: essential, impossible,
The music revealed at the cusp of a breath,
The tumbler that cracks when no one is near,
The muse that shrieks madness at silence
And only whispers under the din.

Listening is

Straightjacket

Breaking orbit from his mother
Somewhere between Shoes and Menswear,
He swerves, this boy.
Around nothing.
Around himself.
Every step half in chasm,
His knees and neck drunk
On the trust of everlasting newness.
His body is a wayward reed,
Green to the core and bending
In the gale of too much stillness,
Too much hush between the glaciers
Of strangers passing with their shopping carts.
Now he is a bullet,
A zombie,
A fighter jet,
A body slam,
A devious whisper
Wandering through racks of empty clothes,
Or a fine new suit, himself:
The man he doesn't yet know
He aims to be,
Already up to his elbows,
Stammering,
Stumbling,
Stretching out
The small shirt of skin,
The vast mind of clay.

Dinner Belles

In flight from the heather,
Her daughters come,
Trains bright yellow
Over the shadowed green,
Scattering waves
Of white and colored wing
In answer to a mother's call.

The soft games left upon the hill,
She recalls from her own stock
Of the passing sky:
The same long days
In the broken breeze
Fostered between ash and pine,
Where a wooden doll met
Every honor she could dream,
Every malady cured by council
With fireflies, and where
The wonder of all the wild realms
Beyond the cattle fence
Lost their heady grip
In the stern promise
Of a second call.

Purpleclip

It would take anyone a lifetime,
Bending it again and again
In search of such precision,
For a spiral as good as this one
Turned by industrial robots
In Zhejiang.

But I'd rather be wrong.
I prefer to imagine it,
This purple-clad paperclip,
As a reed: a straw of latex
Bent by a bent man
Whose Coke-bottle glasses
And gigantic jeweler's lens,
Strapped in tandem around
His patch-bald head,
Tow his nose to the earth
So wherever he goes,
His giant shoes speed
Through a giant's world.

With death-defying grace,
He boldly sips molten steel
Into the elegant twists
And spits a breath of steam.
All for 30 cents a day—
A thousand smoky smiles.
And for this, they call him—
The others in the shop—
Old Dragon.

His wife sits at the next bench,
Pounding out tiny copper bowls
With a tiny ball-peen hammer
Before welding on their spikes.

He sees her scowl each time she hears it—
Old Dragon, Old Dragon—
Perhaps hearing in her mind
The endearment granted her,
Never mentioned directly, of course,
But giggled in English
By the new girls in back
As they feed narrow plastic tubes
With spoons of purple ink,
Despite fresh manicures
And colorful silken scarves,
As if expecting to lure husbands
There on the factory floor,

And they call *her* Tacky.

Representing America

I can apologize,
Mee dee-spee-AH-cheh,
In Italian.

For being a tourist
And for speaking like a child,
My R's flat on every side.

It seemed a better use
Of vocabulary
Than learning questions,
The answers to which
I'd never understand.

Where is the taxi?
Which way to the museum?
The restrooms?

I'm sorry.
I am a tourist.
I speak little Italian
And my tongue is as clumsy
As my nation's leadership.

For which, again,
I am sorry.
The restrooms?

If You Should Be Lost

When the vista glares at you,
And the storefront signs grow harsh,
Their cold buzz refusing to grant
The harbor of their meaning,
You are nearly there.
It is a short drive to the place
Where the path you were expecting,
Now alarmingly late to arrive,
Has been deleted. Move along.

And when the notions of near and far circle
Their wagons against you
Or flatten themselves on the cartoon sky
Like the painted panels behind
A grade-school play,
You may still find your way.
You may still be recognized.

So pass the no-brand fuel
Where county maps are plentiful,
And ignore the kind ol' salt
Riding his tractor along the washboard road—
These are cunning traps.
Continue. Faster.
Until the strange curves
Around mountain and stream
Sing you a brand new story
In a language you didn't know
You would understand.

A little farther
And you will find yourself

Outside your knowing,
Backstage of your being.
In other words, Lost.
Until then, you may still turn back,
Chicken out and find your home
With no artifact, and no harrowing tale
Of chance, escape, or love.
Until then, you may still know who you are
By what you recognize,
Instead of how you arrived.

LOVERS

First Hunger

Confessions tumbling
From mad, wicked skin.
Nubile blood marvelous
With vanity.
Frenzied.
Trembling.
The absurdity of youth
Suffering primordial truth
Through baptism
By carnival.

O Fearsome Darling

I love you so,
That our inevitable divorce
Will be sung in Klingonese,
The street below our window
Running red with trembling curses
And fluttering party clothes.

I love you so,
That our children will go wanting
And wither waiting their turn,
Jostling Daddy for your perfect breasts,
Learning, before they can speak,
To seal their hearts to the world.

I love you so,
That our wedding day
Will bankrupt us financially,
And our wedding night,
In its unsustainable interest,
Morally as well.

I love you so,
That your skin will burn
When I take your hand.
And when I kiss it,
I will leave the most terrible scar
Smoldering in your soul.

I love you so,
That when I lay my eyes on you,
You will flinch at the blow,
Your arms bent up in defense

Of the beam from across the room,
And you will stumble when I blink.

I love you so,
That I go undaunted by your lack of being,
For if God knows what's best for her,
She will paste you in, and soon.
And if God is reluctant to exist,
I may be forced to love her too.

The Tide

Like the jealous ocean
Longing for the fullest moon,
I follow you around the world
Where I'm abandoned in the noon
To take whatever solace
I can find upon the shore,
Until the darkness beckons me
To dream of you once more.

You Compel Me

Perhaps you should sue.
Make the judge condemn me
To return.
Order me to the doctor
So they can check my blood
For signs of affection.
Stick my head in a tube
With magnets and nuclear dye
Lighting my brain red and blue
When I think of you.
Pierce my heart
With the needle of a polygraph
And shine guilty questions
In my eyes.
Pentothal, cudgels,
The crack of a whip,
Pliers, electrodes, a saw:
Undo me nerve by nerve
And scrape away all those parts
Where our love cannot be found
Because I found them first
And carved them away
Like the corners of gristle
Trimmed from the meals
I now make for someone new.

My Tiger

I'll see you soon, my tiger,
Lock eyes with your great cat's glare,
And count the stars reflected
In your wondrous stalking stare.

I'll see you soon, my tiger,
Warm myself in your paws,
Jail myself there, a willing prey,
And smile at your savage claws.

I'll see you soon, my tiger,
Press myself into your fur
To hear the roar of your feral heart
And feel the pulse of your purr.

I'll see you soon, my tiger,
And lose you again without fail—
So says the sly grin as you glide away,
And the flick of your vanishing tail.

The Benefits of Rain

It is raining as if it always has:
A seamless, steady drum
Without a drop of urgency.
So deep a rhythm that I could drown,
Lulled away to sleep
In the middle of the day
Despite the high, tinny drip from the gutters,
And the low grumble,
Ta-ta-te-tapping backbeat
On the picture window by the bed.

As if the day isn't wet enough,
The sound of water in the walls
Tells me my love is under the shower.
When finished muzzling the day,
He enters the room in just a towel,
As if from streaking through the rain—
The towel soaked, no help at all
But for modesty.
I cannot help but smile
As he bends over some deep, internal thought
And sets the wrap aside before spotting me,
Now grinning madly—foolishly—
And glad of it all the rest of the day.

The Art of Loss

A piece at a time or all at once,
Heart broken either way,
We will lose each other somewhere.
Whether we say goodbye
Or learn that we cannot
When news comes overburdened and late,
Every exhalation of breath is merely practice
For the art of loss—
Even when that breath
Is spent with a hidden prayer
For someone who, in leaving,
Has mastered its terrible beauty
At last.

There I Will Shine

Speak to me lightly,
Knowing light is silent only to the ears.
Make of my name an unspoken song
And I will sing to you
Beneath the shiver of your skin.
When we are apart,
I will listen for the sound of your return,
Breath heaving sigh to sigh
Like a kiss whispered across the void,
And answered as quickly
As light dares to fly.

Touch me lightly
As light touches everything in a museum.
Make me into art and test me from afar.
Give me color and then the days
To fade beneath your wash,
A sketch, all pastels,
Made gentle, tender, warm
And safe to place upon your mantle—
Or above your bed—
Where the light in which
I was meant to be seen
Gives me a reason to shine.

DREAMERS

Mission College Carpool

Driving along, he interrupts
With talk of what once occupied
Some plot of land here or there,
And how the names of the roads—
Winchester, Homestead, Forest—all
Once truly meant what they said.
How he came for a high-tech job
When the hills were all dressed
In leather and wool,
The fields still tenderly groomed into garlic
And groves of olive and orange.
Despite his years, his polished career,
He's a cowboy, lost
Among the asphalt and glass,
His face still somehow tan as hide
And as furrowed as his far off fields,
Neck and wrists still mortified
To be cinched up in a white button-down,
His bearish hands still seeking
To soothe their callused pads
On the hilt of a shovel or a saddle's horn
And being pressed to settle instead,
Caught in the glint of a virtual gold rush,
Wrangling only a mouse and keys.

Surrendering September

The mist hangs back,
Crumpled against
The fractured ridge from
Madera to Mt. Umunhum.

Thirty days it waits,
Silvering the sky,
Softening shadows,
And stretching twilight
On its billowing back
Before breaking through
To quench the dust:

The road gone black,
The night gone gray,
And summer simply gone.

The Last Place You Look

It's dirty out there,
As any lost thing will attest:

The lone shoe
Turning her sole to the sky,
Laces splayed frantic and stiff,
Her damp and sticky cushion
A hapless home for something
Longing to bite the absent toe;

Or the mitten,
Whose miles of loping yarn,
Like a chain mail cloud,
Fade from Christmas to Easter
And from herringbone to lint
Now there's no one to tell her
What she mustn't touch—

Both with no notion of a mate
Or any sense of meaning
That isn't mean.
Both hardly worth a glance,
Despite the street-forged fact
That nothing ever starts that way.

Odometer

One hundred thousand miles
Still means something to some:
The kind of milestone met
With a divided heart,
Half in fanfare, half in prayer
That the old American engine
Lasts a little longer,
Not punish us too quickly
For neglecting to reserve
The transplant fund.

I still see all those numbers
Turning at once just past the Pak N Save;
All those nines gone to nothing,
Rolling over the top and then… what?
One hundred thousand one,
One hundred thousand two,
They come and pass the same,
Every mile: just once, here and gone.

Was ninety thousand less deserving?
Or eighty-five? Fifty?
Where was four hundred thirty-three?
What was the number when we met?
When we mingled our CDs?
When we parked
And went into the woods,
Adding mileage to our shoes
And to ourselves;
Turning time into life,
Breath and bone into soul,
And one quiet whisper into love;

Leaning in without a care
For our mismatched numerology,
Ignorant of the decades or days
Until our own hidden hundred-thousands
Wreck our togetherness?

Until then, we are content to pretend
There are no dials. Until the engine sputters,
We are happy to ignore
Which of us is counting forward
All of what is spent,
And which is counting backward
What remains.

That Time

Once in a while she asks:
"Remember that time on the hill?"
And of course I do.
These things may fade and wear,
But just the right amount,
Like long-loved jeans,
Soft and pale as a perfect dream
That just happens to be real.

Lying under the shifting stars,
We could barely keep our hold
Upon the stubble of the green,
The planet slipping underneath,
It's wobble and its spin,
The awesome vaulting rush,
Almost too tangible to bear.

The night was on parade
Because I knew where to look.
As if I were a tamer to the stars,
We watched the rampant Leo
Shake his cindered mane,
Shedding runners white
With broken trains of gold
We thought might strike us down.

But after all the years,
It is the silence, not the show,
I favor in my mind:
The cozy bounty of the stillness,
A feast of intermissions
Between our oohs and aahs.

"When we were first ourselves," I say,
Though I know she needs no answer.
"*That* time on the hill?"

These Doors Lead Back

My world shimmers.
I see it shift in the periphery as I drive,
Or when I turn a corner in my home:
A doorway opens in a patch of grass,
Or a web of pipes fills an open hall
For an instant.
I know it's my eyes—
The world couldn't be so interesting
As when I was a child
Believing in miracles
And monsters.
Still, tenure has taught me
That something lost sometimes returns
If a door is left ajar.
So I pretend to trust
The unshareable as tangible,
And I begin to bless
My aging eyes.

Reborn

I am reborn in moments of surprise,
As when a distant wedge of birds,
Gracing their black V on the cast-washed sky,
Turns white at the edge of a breath,
The arrow of their flight striking
Across a dark green hill.

And while the full thrump
Of my slammed car door
Dims half-ringing in the grocer's lot,
I grapple with a wonder that transcends
My understanding of light and angle
And the coincidence of my wandering gaze.

Because I too trace the line
Between the air and the earth.
I too am dark against the heavens
And bright against the coil.
And I too am free to be transformed,
In the span of a single breath,
By the infinite grace
Of the simplest surprise.

The Flight of Words

On the airplane, we diverge
Like a word hyphenated into
Our separate standby seats,
Mine on the aisle, leading a line,
And his, two rows up and over,
Trapped between parentheses,
Only our parallel trajectories
Linking us to the same story.

In between us, strangers
Are engaged in their business—
As individual words,
Or paired into awkward phrases,
Occasionally bumping each other's privacy
In search of completion,
Intruding and impinging,
But also taking in,
Sampling other words, other phrases,
Alien sounds now on their own lips,
In their own air
Like familiar foreign cognates
Whose peculiar customs are unveiled
In clipped conversations.

After a while, Ceri and I each withdraw:
He to his headphones,
And I to a book of poems—
Easy, digestible, wonderful words
That take me with them
To watch a mouse discover fire
Or a horse doing . . . something—
Just what, I don't recall—

But something noble, or sad;
Something I want to acknowledge,
Though now it's dropping away
As I wander off in the middle of a word,
Fraction of a thought.

Though I lift from the page,
I skim on as mere habit,
Like a gull, gliding low
On an ocean calm,
One wing dipped to stroke
The surface of words,
Testing the water
As if I might join the fish,
And finding it curious,
Too drenched in its own meaning.

Striking higher,
To the clouds of my own internal frontiers,
My shadow falls on the ocean,
Still somehow reading of the horse
While I read the clouds,
As hazy and softly shaded
As the shapes beneath the waves.

Without decision,
I ascend from everything,
Rising through ill defined ramblings,
Unrecognized words
Without conflict
Or context,
Without anything

Except
Perfection.
(   )

Then we're landing—all of us:
The seagull, the plane, my Ceri—
With a cacophony of words all muttered at once
As bookend buildings loom above new roads,
Our concrete punctuation ready
For the meaning we give them,
And us jostling for the order they lend.

We scramble to escape
The flimsy folder of the airframe,
And pour single file into the terminal,
A proper stream of words now—
A parting speech or
A song of broken fellowship—
And disperse again to reclaim our particular verbs,
Our particular purposes,
In our families, our jobs,
Or our particular pleasures.

Finding my Ceri, we join hands,
Forming a tighter than usual dash—
An afterthought to be later absorbed
By our syllables, with no natural idea
As to which comes first and which follows,

Like the gull,
Following the scent of salt,

When the day ends,
Forgets the sea in his nest;

Or the fish,
Fleeing the splintered light of the sun,
At night, in his deep hollow,
Forgets both light and shadow;

Or the sky of perfection,
Shattered by a Daedalus,
When the gravity of words prevails,
Nestles again upon the shoulders of God;

Or the gentle eye,
Reading the poets labor,
With the turning of a page,
Causes the mouse, the horse, and all their deeds
To melt back into merest meme
With only a paper sigh.

WRITERS

Ever Asking

Few questions fall on a poet's ear
That do not land in a verse.
Whether mumbled to death
Or written alive, they cross
To the place where gods
Sleep away their bliss,
Shaking and spent
From spectacular acts
Of creation.

We ask "why are we here?"
In its various states of undress,
And the prose,
Halting or perfect,
Offered in sacrifice
As much as answer,
Is sometimes enough
To rouse the gods to pose
Their own hopeless question—
All of them pulling
At the same aching stake:
"Why are they there, indeed?"

Opportunity for a Poem

A dozen times a day,
A poem comes knocking,
Having climbed the many stairs
From inkling to idea,
Now begging to be inked,
With an apologetic tap
While I'm soaping in the shower,
Rubbing my whole body
In that innocent way of the owner,
Though when the rapping comes,
I am too conscious of my hands,
Slick with suds and maybe
A bit more thorough
Than technically necessary.

The next time the knock comes,
It's small: timid as a child
Put onto it by her mother muse
And told just what to say
When the door opens,
Though with each lingering moment
I nurse my soup to life on the stove
And keep my grilled cheese from catching fire,
She's forgetting every other word—
The ending, the whole point really—
Making it a weird hash at best
If I let her in now.

The next time,
The knock has the fury
Of one waiting all day on the lawn
And noticing the upstairs light go on,

Where I'm startled from the news,
The mail, the comics, the blogs.
But I don't need an angry poem
Raging in with some small splinter of hell
When I'd rather be Googling myself.

So into the night, the knocking comes—
Until the moment I am ready.
Eleven thirty and I sit by the open door,
Poetry books spread from room to room
Like breadcrumbs or bait.
The only tapping now,
The drum of my restless pen on the page,
Empty as the doorway, the stairs and the street.
Empty as the eleventh hour for want of a stay.
Empty but for the scrap
I finally find beneath the welcome mat—
The little note that reads:
A dozen times a day,
A poem comes knocking.

Aunt Nora's Gift to Poetry

Is wit really an excuse—
Or even your proven superiority—
For a two-thousand-word review
That barely touches on her book?

Dull, you say. Dull
As those summers Aunt Nora
Took you to the ocean cottage
(Not the ocean, but the cottage)
And kept you bottled there
For fear that you would drown.
As if you'd be fool enough
To leap into the surge,
Kick out to the current
And drift away, waving happily
To the strange toy house on the shore
And its frantic porcelain doll.

I suppose, if it was really dull,
That's all I'd need to know,
And be thankful I was spared
The name of a single poem.
At least in my review,
I acknowledge dear Aunt Nora,
Though I see her trading gossip
With her flush-cheeked neighbor, Meg,
When she sent you outside
To stop you jumping on the couch,
Leaving no one at all to watch
Your tired, chilly voyage
Down the coast and out to sea.

Vacation

The inkling mopes around,
Grows up an impulse
And sets up a dirty shop,
A persistent nagging
That this has gone too far—
This whole business with words.

There should be days,
Maybe even weeks without
Catching sight of their squiggles
Marching in formation—
Lines of literary ants
Working the corpse
Of some sweet symbol.
Stretches where the tooth of the page,
The hooks and spines of letters,
Saw other minds than mine,
Rasp on other tongues.

Go ahead, says this rough idea,
Tape a sign on the door and walk away—
A sign the muse is sure to understand:
One that says
Absolutely nothing.

Sabbatical

For the muse,
The advantages of being a goddess,
And more than a little wild:
There's no mention of desertion,
No notice of vacation or return,
No need to take a change of dress
Or buy a ticket for the train
Where the many haggard riders,
Merely watching her pass by,
Grow pensive, silent, strange,
And slip away to make their mark
On paper, canvas,
Concrete, or flame,
But all of them more brightly,
Spreading the hint
Of her blazing glance and knowing smile
In every brilliant thing they do,
And not a one, not ever,
Daring strike a conversation—
Too busy with some new insight
To wonder where she's bound.

Please

Say something that shouldn't be new:
Words made warm from their waiting.

Speak of things that ache
With the burden of their beauty,
That strain to burst the seams of their script
And wet the wandering ear
With a passably puckish breath.

Say death. Say mother.
Say father. Say horse.
Say night and laughter
Or day and despair.
Say everything sideways
As if from a rolling dream,
Yet mean it more than one can say.

Say it without the blessing of the muse.
Steal her most accidental murmur
Like a kiss of righteous ripeness
From a world more real than ours:
Where the bliss of words
All ringing at once
Is more than we can otherwise bear.

Say it. Say it now.

Spotlight

I like being studied. I like being *studied*.
I have a medical curiosity,
And I have this need to be
What my psychiatrist sees.
Oh, I *like* being studied.

The other day, I went to the doc.
He was just too cool in that long, white frock.
I told him about my pineal gland.
I said "listen, doc, it's gotten way out of hand.
Deep into the future, that's what I see,
And y'know lately it's kinda been bothering me."
He poked and he prodded
From my tongue to my balls,
Then he slipped away quietly
To make some phone calls.
(I like being studied.)

Good ol' doc sent me to the shrink.
I claimed his couch and we started to link.
The purest in symbiotic scrutiny:
I lie to him, and he lies to me.
"Yes, Mother's a bitch. Yes, Father's a bore."
But when the hour is up, we both know the score:
Two hundred bucks on my way out the door . . .
"See ya next week?"
Oh yeah! We both want some more.
'Cuz we're being studied.

But today I got a ring
So I picked up the phone:
It's those insurance geeks!
God, I wish they'd leave me alone—
"You used my lifetime allowance by age forty-one.
We want our card back:
Today, man! You're done
Being studied."

So now I'm a poet—
Less out-of-pocket expense—
Just a ham on a cord,
Though I mean no offense.
I just want to open your ears
And dip your brains in my song
And extract the reaction
Before you feel anything's wrong.

When the mic has gone dead
And I swim from the stage
I'll skinny-dip in your blankness,
Wade through your love,
Drink your rage.
It's the spotlight sickness,
Nothing poetically new.
I just like being studied.
How about you?

Catering to the Muse

The jar rings under the butter knife:
A demented dinner bell,
The tone dry and tasteless,
The blade angry and clean,
The last dregs of mustard
Plowed aside to leave
The thinnest furrows of transparency
Behind the label on the glass.

But at this late hour,
There is no proper place
A man in his underwear
May acquire a new jar.
So I ring the jar
And scrape the jar
And damn the jar
And refuse to draw any analogy
To my life.

It's just for a sandwich.
Whatever *mustard* shares with *muse*
Is pure coincidence—
I'll take my turkey dry.
But I will also slide the jar,
Empty as sin and superstition,
Back into the fridge.

One never knows what's sacred
In the larder of the muse.

& OTHER CURIOUS BEASTS

The Lion on the Bus

A man is yelling on the bus.
Someone passed him by
Without meeting his wild gaze.
The slight, worse than a snarl,
Breaks the cage of his voice,
And once free, it roars.

Though I am as pained
As the other riders
Whose two dollar fare
Now seems too much,
I notice in the howl
The way each shriek
Falls pinched in apology.

The next stop is quite popular,
But now I'm curious.
I stare back as the cowards leave.
"What you looking at?"
The wild man barks,
But I just grin, showing teeth,
And he, tucking his tail, understanding,
Gets off with all the rest.

I Want What I Want

"They Knew What They Wanted,"
  —John Ashbery

I accuse my parents.
I am an American soldier.
I am a fugitive from a chain gang.
I am curious.

I am David. I am Dina.
I am legend. I am the law.
I am not what you want.
I am trying to break your heart.

I can do bad all by myself.
I can get it for you wholesale.
I can hear the sea.
I can't go home.

I dreamed of Africa.
I drink your blood. I eat your skin.
I hate Valentine's Day.
I haven't got a hat.

I hired a contract killer.
I kiss your hand, Madame.
I know where I'm going!
I love you too.

I shot Andy Warhol.
I step through Moscow.
I wake up screaming.
I wanna hold your hand.

I want a dog. I want to live!
I was born, but . . .
I was a teenage Frankenstein.
I woke up early the day I died.

I'll cry tomorrow.
I'll sleep when I'm dead.
I'm gonna git you sucka.
I've heard the mermaids singing.

Shaving in Peace

The giddiness of ramshackle thunder
Follows the boys upstairs;
Jake topping two at a time,
Just out of sync with Van and John,
Shrieking and creaking—
Boys and banisters, both—
The dog weaseling his way
Underneath and between,
The chittering clash of prickly paws
Unsure on the polished wood.
Even the kitchen pottery barks,
The chandelier shaking its head
To make the shadows dance
To the boys' barbarian beat.

Accusations and denial
Pour through the floor in waves,
Each crest seemingly capped
With a double body slam,
A stuttering storm
That dulls to a roar
As the devil is drained
One triumph or tear at a time,
Till soothed and slow,
The blissful respite of three still boys—
A tender trio of angels,
For a moment nearly forgotten—
Wakes the hair on the back of my neck
Just in time to spare the dog
A calamitous tonsure.

Under the Florescent Hum

The kitchen can't be seen.
The smallness is so immense
That the appliances have become
Drunken boxers, throwing doors
Like wild punches at the referee
Trying for a soda
And scorching an elbow
While the oven cools,
Ticking its metal tongue,
One yellow eye glaring at the sink
Burbling back over it's spawn.
The sooty mildew
Seeps from its soggy belly
While the refrigerator sulks:
"Not mine," it lies,
Smacking the slanted seal
Of its own moldy lips,
Slowly losing its cool,
Its inner light long, long dead.

Spring Lambs

"Yea, Though I Walk"
  —Virginia Hamilton Adair

We come slowly up
The only road to town,
Feeling for the broken hedge—
The broken path that cuts away
Between the vineyards
And the grazing fields
Now puffed with lambs at play.
Their abandon on the hillside
Leaves it pocked and plain,
Its new flowers now
Bent and broken on the earth.

Meadow Blossom

When the terror vaults,
She tries to follow:
Over the dogs,
Over the fence,
And even over the moon.
Despite appearances—
Despite lack of any name
But *sheep*—
It isn't resignation
That brings her back into her blood:
She is driven there
By the quick close of teeth
To retreat into her bones, their marrow,
And pursued even there by nose and claw,
To the threshold of the final field
Where the sounds of gnashing and gnawing
Become a kind of music,
And where the muffled throb
Of the foiled heart
Becomes a nuisance—
Though one that fades
With a further canine blessing,
Leaving her unfurled so far beyond the stars,
A goddess looking back
On the spreading meadow blossom
Dividing the cubs from the lambs,
Understanding
She could not have accomplished this
Alone.

Mew!

Kylie mews at his water dish.
I fill it and he's happy.

He mews at his food dish.
I feed him and he's thrilled.

He mews over a shoelace.
I tease him and he's delighted.

He mews from the middle of the room.
I have no idea what he wants.

Neither does he.
He trots away as if to say,

"Well, it was worth a try."

The Whispers of Wolves

The fantastic languages
Of ghosts and gods
Reward drunkenness,
Impure faith,
And a gypsy heart
Where delirium translates
For wolves and crows,
Roadside satyrs,
Magician's longings,
And all manner and bearing
Of flames.

Ooo

It is not, after all, a car alarm.
It is merely a cow on the greening hill
At the top of the street,
Lowing. Which is shy of bellowing.
So neither car alarm nor cow alarm,
But if cows can be said to sing,
She is singing
One mild, cow note, repeatedly.

On the hill, not grazing,
But softly singing,
She is a lone cow:
A singular rectangle,
or its crude approximation;
One lumpy, bright white flag
With balloon-string legs, hovering
Over a ragged shadow.

At this distance, *moo* is merely *ooo*.
It's not a lonely call, nor
Noticeably happy, hungry, or horny.
It's nothing that would stay with me
When I close my door, except
In league with the light:
The magic-hour, pre-sunset light.
It sets her aglow,
Her frame softly haloed,
Her song now softly hallowed,
An ungulate prayer,
Waiting for cosmic favor.

Not for food or shelter.
Not for a mate.
Just notice. The same
As we all crave:
To have a moment
In the eyes of God,
Singular, glowing,
Singing out in this beautiful place,
And despite the crudeness of our bearing,
Be seen, like the cow,
To make it Majestic.

Exploring Heaven

Meadow is the word:
Green and perfect,
The cure for a fear
That's gone before
The hush can reveal it.

The remarkable peace
From atop the hill
Runs down into nothing
Until I recall that
Valley is the word:
Squares of tillage,
Stands of pine,
With small white blocks—
Home is the word
For the one that is mine,
Just down the road.

Though in the other direction—
That place I am heading—
Is a field of horses,
Wild as the wind
But for one,
Already watching,
Already hoping
To take me away,
Faithful and unafraid,
To the edge of everything
And back again.

And the word for that,
At the top of my map,
I could never have understood
Before now.

 Harry Lafnear

is an award winning poet and showcased poetry performer.

has been featured on *IndieFeed Performance Poetry,*
Cloudy Day Art, The Slam Idol, and *PoetGuru* podcasts,
BZoO Worldwide Radio Online, and Nils Peterson's
Poet Laureate blog.

is the creator of *The Everyday Muse* podcast, has co-written
numerous commercial video games, worked with the UARS
satellite team at the University of Michigan, and run a Las
Vegas sign shop.

is a Poetry Center San José board member, serving as Assistant
Treasurer and as Publications Chair.

is an organizing member of the Willow Glen Poetry Project.

is a technical publications expert and graphic designer by trade.

lives in Milpitas, California with his spouse, Steve.

9245842R0

Made in the USA
Charleston, SC
24 August 2011